THE BEST GIFT A DAD

ILLUSTRATOR GRACE DYKES

AUTHOR TONY BORELLI

 ISBN: 978-0-578-45047-6

AUTHOR ACKNOWLEDGEMENTS

Thanks first and foremost to Jesus Christ, through whom all things are possible and through whom anyone and anything can be redeemed.

In November of 2016, I passed out in the hallway of my home, my head blasting a hole in the wall. Over the next week, my body repeatedly felt like it was completely shutting down. As I would later learn, it was because my heart was stopping. Several times I felt like I was about to die. The solution was the implementation of a pacemaker. While the surgery is relatively common and is less complicated than other heart-related procedures, there is no doubt in my mind that it was a life-saver for me. Getting a pacemaker was a second lease on life. One of the main reasons I composed this book was to make sure I capitalized on my second chance and ensured my kids had documented proof about how I felt about them and what was important to me. Thanks to Dr. David DeLurgio for performing my surgery, to my cardiologist Dr. Hunter Champion and his colleague Kyle Cullefer, and to my personal, round-the-clock physician, my wife Liz.

Just four and a half years prior, our family had a health scare that was just as frightening and much greater in length. After a difficult and complicated pregnancy, Liz gave birth – five weeks premature – to our twins, Jackson and Natalie. Jackson came home after just two weeks in the NICU, but Natalie needed four months, plus surgeries to repair strictures in her aorta and colon. Thank you to the countless medical professionals at both Piedmont Columbus Regional and Children's Healthcare of Atlanta, including but certainly not limited to surgeons Dr. Paul Kirshbom and Dr. Matthew Clifton.

Thanks to my niece, Grace Dykes (a.k.a. "Gracie"), for accepting the challenge to produce the illustrations for this book, and for doing such a great job! Thanks also to her parents, Shane and Christine Dykes, for their support, and once again, to Liz for suggesting that I ask Gracie in the first place. We love you, Gracie!

Thanks to everyone at our family's church home, Church on the Trail (formerly known as MyChurch) of Columbus, Georgia, including founding and current pastors Jeff Murphy and Ed Grifenhagen, respectively. Thanks to the staff of the youth program for what they have already invested in our two children and for allowing me to be a part of their team. Thanks to Kyndal Nipper and Keli Vernon for welcoming me aboard, to our former director, Brooke Saalman, for whom I have great respect (#saalmanstrong), and to our current director, Allison Judah, for all that she does.

I could talk endlessly about all who have supported me through the years from St. Michael's in Auburn, my church home in college and for several years thereafter. For brevity's sake, I'll give a shout out to Matt and Michelle Schultz and to Bob and Carolyn Norton for all the students they have welcomed with open arms into their homes over the years, providing invaluable guidance; to Ashley Dupuis for her pointers on book publishing (check out her book, Night Night Wishes); and most of all to Eddie Victoria, whose many great deeds over the years was topped by his transporting me to the 1997 Auburn-Georgia football game in Athens and introducing me to his sister, then a Georgia student and now my wife Liz. War Eagle!

Thanks to my parents, Patrick and Barbara Borelli, for all they have done for me over the years, and to my sister, Belinda Manuel, and her husband, Chris.

Last and of course not least, thanks yet again to Liz and to Jackson and Natalie. You are the best family anyone could ask for. I am so proud of you and I love you all very much!

Tony Borelli

TO THE DAD

No matter your walk of life, your role as a father is unquestionably one of the most important assignments you will ever have. While your child may technically belong to you for the time being, he or she actually belongs eternally to God; He has entrusted you with his or her care for just a little while. Your mission is to help bring your son or daughter home, for them to ultimately spend eternity in Heaven with God.

The stakes are high, and statistically speaking, no one is more qualified to assist your child in this quest than you. Many articles cite data that the father's commitment to Jesus is the most crucial factor in determining the commitment the family's children will have to Christ as they mature. One such article, by Jack Wellman[1], states, "The importance of children coming to saving faith in Jesus Christ can be broken down like this: 7% of saved children will help lead both of their parents to faith in Jesus Christ. 23% of saved wives and mothers will help lead their husbands and children to faith in Jesus Christ. 94% of saved husbands and fathers will help lead their entire family to faith in Jesus Christ."

As a father of 6-year-old twins, I don't claim to have all the answers, and this book is not intended to be the irrefutable, all-encompassing guide on how to raise children to be disciples of Christ. Rather, it is intended to be a starting point in the discussion.

"The Best Gift a Dad Can Give" was written for a target audience of 2nd through 5th graders, but is equally applicable to sons and daughters of any age. Even if your children are younger, it is never too early to begin talking with them about some of the principles described. Conversely, if they are already in 6th grade or older and you have rarely if ever spoken with them about Christ, starting a discussion about Jesus today is always better than putting it off until tomorrow or never having it at all. And if you've already talked about Jesus in your home, great! My hope is that this book will help augment and strengthen what you have already established.

As you spend time with your child reading this book, don't hesitate to interject with your own opinions, experiences, and examples as you wish, tailoring the conversation to be unique to your family and your individual and collective circumstances. Again, this book aims to be a discussion-starter. By the same token, if you are more comfortable with just reading the book and letting your child ask questions as you go along, that works as well. The bottom line is to create a situation where you and your child are most comfortable talking about Jesus and talking about the role you will each play in helping each other get to Heaven!

Thank you so much, and may God bless you and your family.

Tony Borelli

(1) http://www.patheos.com/blogs/christiancrier/2013/07/29/the-importance-of-good-christian-fathers/

I am SO proud to be your father! I love you, and I will always be your #1 fan no matter what. Because of this, I want to give you THE BEST GIFT a father can ever give his child.

"[The Father] guarded him as the apple of his eye."

Deuteronomy 32:10

What is the best gift a dad can give? Is it the latest and greatest awesome toy? Or video game? Is it a phone? A car? A new pet? A ticket to a concert or game?

"Every good and perfect gift is from above, coming down from the Father of the heavenly lights, who does not change like shifting shadows."

James 1:17

CR
AY
ONS

No, THE BEST GIFT a father can give his child is doing all he can to ensure they both have a relationship with JESUS CHRIST that is as strong as possible!

While it has been two thousand years since Jesus walked the Earth, we know His story through the Bible. It is a proven fact in history that many people, including most of his original disciples, willingly died for their belief that Jesus was truly the Son of God.

"For the wages of sin is death, but the gift of God is eternal life in Christ Jesus our Lord."

Romans 6:23

God loves you more than anyone else does. He created you and died on the cross for your sins, so that if you believe in Him, you will go to Heaven.

You and I will spend infinitely more time at our eternal destination than we do here on Earth. So making sure that you and I spend all of that time in Heaven is the most important thing I can do!

That is why THE BEST GIFT that I can give you is a commitment to the two of us giving our lives to Jesus, and to both of us putting our faith and trust in Him.

"For my Father's will is that everyone who looks to the Son and believes in him shall have eternal life, and I will raise them up at the last day."

John 6:40

But what does that mean?

It means that even when it seems that nothing else is right, we can still be truly happy. His sacrifice for us on the cross is already more than we deserve, and it should be enough for us to be full of joy.

It means that based on the example of Jesus (as told in the Bible), our three goals on Earth should be to 1) improve the world, 2) improve the lives of others, and 3) enjoy our time on Earth (while staying true to the example of Jesus).

"The earth is the Lord's, and everything in it, the world, and all who live in it."

Psalm 24:1

It means that we know that happiness is more plentiful when we live to help others than when we live only for ourselves, and that we act accordingly.

It means that with each hour of each day, we hear One Voice above all voices: the Voice of God.

It means that with each thing that we do, we live our lives for an Audience of One: Jesus.

"A voice of one calling: 'In the wilderness prepare the way for the Lord.'"

Isaiah 40:3

It means that no matter what friends, classmates, or others might say, we commit to doing and saying what Jesus wants us to do or say, even if it's not popular with others.

It means that when people disagree with our decision to follow what Jesus says (instead of doing what they say), we realize those people will only be around us for a short while, but our time in Heaven will be forever.

"Am I now trying to win the approval of human beings, or of God? Or am I trying to please people? If I were still trying to please people, I would not be a servant of Christ."

Galatians 1:10

It means that we lead people to do good things, rather than follow people that do bad (or do nothing).

It means telling friends about Jesus and teaching others what He has done for us.

It means that we always tell the truth and that we always keep trying! It means never giving up, no matter what!

It means both of us showing your mother tremendous love and respect.

"Jesus looked at them and said, 'With man this is impossible, but not with God; all things are possible with God.'"

Mark 10:27

It means continuously reading and studying the Bible to learn more and more about God.

It means praying to God to ask for His help and His forgiveness, while also letting Him lead us to do what He wants us to do.

It means you and me working as a team to reach all of these goals. It means correcting each other along the way to make sure we get back on track and reach our ultimate destination: Heaven!

I am committed to working with you as a team to do all of this. This is truly THE BEST GIFT that I can ever give! I love you!

"For where two or three gather in my name, there am I with them."

Matthew 18:20

50365149R00015

Made in the USA
Columbia, SC
05 February 2019